THE JOHN CAGE EXPERIENCES

T0116708

THE JOHN CAGE
experiences

8 SOLOS, DUOS OR TRIOS (WITH THINGS)

VINCENT THOLOMÉ

Translated from the French by Alex Niemi

Autumn Hill Books
Bloomington, Indiana

AHB

This is an Autumn Hill Books book
Published by Autumn Hill Books, Inc.
1138 E. Benson Court
Bloomington, IN 47401
USA

First published as *The John Cage Experiences*
© 2007 by Le Clou dans le fer

This book has benefitted greatly from the support of the Collège des traducteurs de Seneffe | Passa Porta.

Design and layout by Justin Angeles

ISBN: 9780998740058
Library of Congress Control Number: 2018963855

*Æ*B
www.autumnhillbooks.org

to éric jaques
maja jantar

and,
of course,
sebastian dicenaire

CONTENTS

The red (and chrome) race car (*for the entire experience john cage or his equivalent will drive one of those little race cars with a mechanical motor you recharge by rolling the wheels rapidly backwards several times in a row on a table or maybe even the ground*)

In 1935. John cage regularly drives around the Arizona desert in a red and chrome race car. He regularly caresses the hot steering wheel with his hand when he crosses the hot and frankly boiling Arizona desert at top speed. In 1935. In the Arizona desert. Tons of dust rise into the air as john cage goes by. When. John cage. In 1935. In the Arizona desert. Hears the purring

(here john cage or his equivalent rolls the race car on the table or the floor 5 times)

motor of his race car. He loses his train of thought and. Frankly. Loses himself in his

(here john cage or his equivalent rolls the race car on the table or the floor 2 times)

black hole. John cage says. Later. John cage says later. In 1935. John cage has a red and chrome race car bought secondhand for less than $200. He also possesses an equally large and beautiful hole in his head. So that. Each time each time each time. In the Arizona desert. Taking off at top speed. Raising tons of dust as it goes by. The red and chrome race car loses john cage in his thoughts inside of his black hole. In fact. Inside his race car. The

(in fact john cage or his equivalent can wait before rolling his race car whatever he wants but he should

do it 4 times on the table on his hand or on the floor
to wind up the mechanical motor)

heat of the desert does not eat away at john cage. The heat of the Arizona desert doesn't redden his fingers. Doesn't frost or liquefy john cage or the windows inside the race car. Frankly. The Arizona heat. The stifling heat of the Arizona desert. Is having a lot of trouble getting inside the race car. The air conditioning in john cage's red and chrome race car. In 1935. Is amazing. So the heat gives up. Anyone other than john cage would fall asleep at the wheel crossing the arid plains of the Arizona desert. Anyone. Even john cage. Would have. From rubbing elbows with the Arizona steppes in 1935 like john cage. A strong inner experience. Maybe. Instead of being in a red and chrome race car. John cage would feel the effects of the heat more

(roll on the table surely but on the whole table or only
one part of it on the whole floor or only a part of it? at
any rate roll 1 time)

on a horse. Maybe john cage wouldn't ask himself questions about the meaning of life or the meaning of a black hole in his head on a horse. Luckily john cage is in a red and chrome race car crossing through one of the vast and scorched Arizona plains at top speed. Tons of swirling dust sting the car body. After all the summer road trips an auto body mechanic will cover the beautiful race car in anti-corrosive. John cage

(at any rate roll 2 times on his hand)

tends to the body of his race car in fall. Meanwhile. In the summer. You might say john cage plays at chasing the dusts of the desert. Meanwhile. He clears the roads of every municipality in Arizona. That would be a neat job he thinks in 1935. However. Soon. In one or two minutes something incredible will happen to john cage. He will meet the strong heat of the Arizona desert. He will almost die of dehydration he says. Actually in one or two minutes john cage's beautiful red car will make the acquaintance of a blue aluminum car. At an intersection. In one or two minutes john cage's red and chrome race car will end its days on the great plains of Arizona. However. The death of his race car will not move john cage. Focused on the task at hand john cage will not even turn around one last time. When he travels the road on foot. On the carcass of his race car. He will be so busy lending a hand to the beautiful driver of the blue aluminum car. He will be so busy

(at any rate roll without winding up the mechanical motor and do it 2 times)

employing his charming beautiful smile. Later. Yes. He'll think of his red and chrome race car. Later he'll unquestionably miss his red and chrome race car. Meanwhile. John cage and the beautiful driver of the blue aluminum car need to get somewhere on foot. Meanwhile. They don't clutch each other as tightly as they would on the vast plains of Mongolia. However. Even though they don't clutch each other as tightly as they would on the vast plains of Mongolia. The heat doesn't separate them all that much. Actually what a neat guy this john cage is thinks the future mrs. john cage. Thank god I dug up a rare gem. The kind my mother dreamed about in her time. Thinks the future mrs. john cage. Another time. Much later. John cage will wonder which hands dismantled his red and chrome race car. What. For example. Would they do with the recycled car body. How many children will swing inside its Michelin tires. Or Goodyear. Most likely Goodyear. Probably Goodyear. Supposing that. In 1935. Goodyear tires. Or Michelin. Or Michelin. Exist. Are circulated around the world like in Arizona. Like in Arizona. Millions of vehicles. Millions of race cars. Red and chrome. Red and chrome. But I don't know. That I don't know. I don't remember. John cage. The composer. Thinks later. John cage thinks thinking of his red race car. John cage thinks wondering which generator his powerful diesel engine is a part of. Will chickens have laid eggs on its seats. Etc. Etc. All things like that. All the things like that in john cage's head. In john cage's black hole. The composer. Incapable. In 1935. Like later on for that matter. Of losing his temper at a woman. All the same she ruined his race car. Let's not forget. Let's not. I know a lot of guys. John cage will say. I know a lot of older guys who would've raked her over the coals for that. Ha ha. He says. Ha ha. Now the red race car is stripped down. And he john cage must live the rest of his days with that. His dearest. He says. Later. His dearest. What a life.

(at any rate push the race car to see if it will go by itself and do it 4 times)

The hotel room *(during the duration of the experience john cage or his equivalent will stretch his arm desperately toward a bedside lamp that is real and illuminated but nevertheless unreachable)*

We wonder what john cage has in his head. We also wonder what he's really thinking about. After walking many many kilometers. In 1935. In the Arizona desert. John cage. And the future mrs. cage. The fiancée of mr. cage. A superb woman. Certainly. At that point in time. In a baby doll nightdress. Well. They arrive at a hotel. They take a room in a hotel. With a bed. One bed. For two. Wow. It's. Yes. Sex. It's. Yes. Very hot. Very hot between john cage and the future mrs. cage. But. After a frugal meal. And even though it's very hot very sexy between john cage and the future mrs. cage. We wonder why john cage. Once in his

(john cage or his equivalent meaning anybody you or me stretches an arm desperately towards a bedside lamp that is real and illuminated and if the rendering of the experience is done sitting down at the far end of the table)

bed. After his ablutions. Once the covers are pulled tightly up to his armpits. Stretches his right arm out desperately to turn off the hotel bedside lamp. We wonder why john cage. Comfortably stretched out on his bed. In pale blue pajamas like for example something very ugly very old-fashioned it's shocking. Doesn't just ask his future wife who's still awake at this hour. Still her time. For. Ablutions. To turn off

the hotel bedside lamp when she comes soon. In
5 minutes. Max. To

*(the effort that it costs to stretch out an arm is clearly
visible on the face of john cage or his equivalent
anyway we see it if the rendering of the experience is
done sitting down... if the rendering of the experience
takes place lying down all the effort will be visible in
the body of john cage or his equivalent writhing
desperately to reach this damn lamp)*

sleep. To join in fact her. Yes. Fiancé. Let me put
it to you this way. In fact. We wonder a lot of
things on the subject of john cage a man like
everyone else meaning like you and me like you
and me. It appears looking as we do here in detail
at john cage's reasons for being and for acting
that there is in john cage's head like in

*(if everything takes place lying down the body of john
cage or his equivalent should render the effort
without moving too much john cage's experience
being as mental as it is physical)*

anybody's head a black hole. Well. Then. What I
mean is. We notice for example how carefully
john cage smoothed the sheets and the blanket
such that john cage is now perfectly ensconced
in a creaseless sarcophagus in his hotel room.
The

(here for a little variety, maybe attempt 2 quick
punches in the direction of the lamp)

wallpaper in the room is tearing at the rate of 1
mm per year. Once the drapes are drawn. They
don't let in a single sound from the street. Not a
single tire screech for example. Not a single
drinking song bellowed by a drunkard. So that.
We

(a small spasm towards the lamp and that's it)

can say that. In the hotel room. John cage and the
future mrs. cage. Human beings. All the same.
Like you and me. Like you and me. Well. They
live yes as if in the shadow of an experience. They
live an experience withdrawn from the world. So
that. Everything that happens in shadow.
Everything that happens in the hotel room. Well.
Yes. Assumes. John cage thinks. Suddenly
nervous. A considerable importance. So that.
John cage thinks. Suddenly nervous. There is
something. In this experience. Something. Yes.
Good. To get out of it. Without a doubt. Without
a doubt. Thinks john cage. The composer. The

(take care separating the words and gestures to let
each live in turn and have a space where it can stretch
out comfortably thinks john cage or his equivalent)

musician. So that. She. The future mrs. cage. A superb woman. That goes without saying. Passes. Phew. Very sexy. Very sexy. By the foot of the bed in a baby doll nightdress. She is vigorously pulling hair from a brush when john cage sees her pass by the foot of the bed. She even hums a popular tune. And why not something by louis armstrong. It is 1935. After all. After all. She still has things to do in the bathroom. Thinks john cage. The composer. When his future. His. Yes. Already. Already. Promised. Vigorously. Passes by the foot of the bed. She pounds the ground.

(barely moving here)

Literally. Her feet are bare and she is hammering the ground. And while the future mrs. cage returns to the bathroom. While john cage is wrapped tightly in the sheets and. Desperately. Stretching his arm. The left or the right. Not so important in the end. Not so important. In view of. Yes. Reaching the hotel bedside lamp. In fact its switch. Then turning it off. A clump of hair flies

(here move the hand once and then that's it)

gracefully into the trash. The wool threads of the full carpet stand up straight. The wallpaper continues to tear. A truck outside backs into a streetlamp. It can't be heard from the room. It could be guessed from the dimming light intensity of the electric bulb but john cage. Absorbed in his thoughts. And in his actions as well. In fact. Doesn't notice. No. So that. Yes. John cage's life in the hotel room is now a dearest future wife doing something bad but what at the bathroom sink. The wallpaper tears imperceptibly in the upper right corner of the room. The feeling of being the object of an experience but what kind. So that. Once a future mrs. cage has finished with the bathroom. Once a future mrs. cage. Very sexy. In a baby doll nightdress. In a baby doll nightdress. Carefully closes the bathroom door. Once the heels of the future mrs. cage skirt the bed. So

(and here john cage or his equivalent gets up from the chair or stands up goes and turns off the lamp that has been illuminated throughout the entire experience then comes back to either sit in the chair or lie down on the ground concluding the experience)

that. Now. The future mrs. cage. Superb. Really hot. In a baby doll nightdress. She disturbs the bed's careful organization. The smooth sheets without a single crease. She. Yes. John cage thinks. Oui. Slides under the. Yes. Oui. Sheets. Like it was nothing. Like it was nothing. Thinks john cage. Who observes her. Without saying anything. From his sarcophagus. From the cozy nest concocted in his bed. Slides yes maybe under the sheets maybe without turning off. Without turning off. The. Yes. Bedside lamp. Unattainable. Out of john cage's. Reach. Unless with a superhuman. Effort. On his part. By him. John cage. A man. Like anyone. Like you and me. Thinks john cage. From his black hole. From the hole he has. Like anyone. In his head. Somewhere. He thinks. Obliged as he is to get up. To leave the bed. Just to turn off. After all. After all. John cage will think. In old-fashioned pajamas. She's gone too far. She's gone too far. That's all. That's all that there is to say. That's all there is to say about john cage. That's all that there is to say about john cage at the hotel. About the beautiful and terrible. Very hot. Very sexy. Experience of john cage at the hotel. In 1935. In Arizona. He will specify. Nothing to add. Later. Much later. Yes.

THE JOHN CAGE EXPERIENCES

The acme store *(during the experience john cage or his equivalent will sit on a wooden chair and remain silent and immobile throughout the experience while an associate does the commentary)*

*(the experience begins with john cage or his
equivalent meaning anybody man or woman in fact
even a child sitting on a simple wooden chair with a
straight back and why not their hands flat on their
thighs)*

In 1935. After some crazy very hot very sexy
nights in a hotel in Arizona. Mr. john cage
marries mrs. john cage. In 1935 there is an acme
store selling vacuum cleaners on the corner of
john cage's street. In 1935 mrs. john cage moves
to a new apartment in New York City. The fact is
that mrs. cage. The wife of mr. cage. In 1935.
Frankly. Isn't moving into an apartment in New
York City alone. Some machines are already
playing in mr. and mrs. cage' apartment but not a
vacuum cleaner. The fact is that

*(as will be the case throughout the entire experience
the commentary is interrupted leaving just john cage
or his equivalent sitting immobile and silent on his
chair remember a simple wooden chair)*

when he goes to the acme store alone in 1935 john
cage means to buy a machine. John cage's wife
stayed home alone in john cage's apartment and is
playing with her machines. An electric stove
equipped with buttons. A coffeemaker with a dial.
John cage's wife maintains good relations with her
machines but unfortunately not with washing

machines or vacuum cleaners. So in 1935 the wife of john cage sends john cage to buy something. A machine. A washing machine at the acme store. So when john cage enters the acme store he says firmly he thinks washing machine. However he says a strange thing happens to john cage once he's in the acme store. Even though john cage is ready as anybody to make

(in this experience the difficulty will be letting the silence run long enough to establish itself maybe the solution would be to determine its length by chance by throwing dice for example)

his request the fact is that john cage draws a blank. Say the tongue of john cage enters a black hole. Let's remember that john cage has a black hole in his head like anybody like you and me. The essential

(it goes without saying that these lengths will be determined before the experience before john cage or his equivalent takes their spot on the wooden chair sitting up straight and why with their hands placed flat on their thighs yes)

experience of john cage in 1935 at the acme store rests on the fact that john cage's tongue enters his black hole. Ensuring that. The essential part of john cage's experience at the acme store takes place in silence. Even if you can easily find different models of push-button washing machines in the corners of the acme store in 1935. Even if it's easy for john cage to formulate his request. It's that john cage. The composer. A man of noise. Of sound. And words. Like anybody. Anybody. Well. It's that john cage. Well. Yes. Well. He doesn't know why. He never figured out why. The fact is that. In 1935. At the acme store. He literally lets himself get literally pushed around. So that. Even though john

(however we shouldn't use more than two dice we shouldn't throw a length of time greater than 12 seconds or fewer than 2 seconds)

cage has not yet formulated any request and though he won't formulate any request. They. Someone. Presents him with a vacuum for lack of anything better. The man in question. They. Someone. Shows him its features. Literally mind-blowing. Literally mind-blowing. John cage will say. Later. At home. To his wife. About a vacuum. They tell him how much faster and farther he can go. They prove to him by a + b the advantage of having no lever or pedal. Then they spend a lot of time waiting for. John cage himself. To produce an opinion. A

(maybe we should be careful to ensure however that two similar lengths do not follow one another)

desire. A need. His silence becomes uncomfortable. In fact it's uncomfortable that john cage's tongue may be. Well. Literally in his black hole. In fact nobody can see it. In fact they suspect an attack or a degeneration. In fact they continue more or less as if it were nothing. A speck of dust. In the acme store in 1935. Floats in a ray of light. An unknown insect lands on the window. The air conditioning is on. They're wearing the acme store uniform. Most of the clients come as a couple. Over the course of the year. Mr. and mrs. john cage have acquired an electric stove equipped with buttons and a coffeemaker with a dial. In 1935 mr. and mrs. john cage like everybody want. And possess. More and more. A miniscule scratch in the parquet floor. Well. Abruptly comes to john cage's

(with the experience in progress it's most natural to follow the duration of the lengths by the crocodile method 1 crocodile equals 1 second 2 crocodiles equals 2 seconds etc. so that during the silence john cage's associate or his equivalent mentally and slowly recites the number of crocodiles drawn at random then she or he begins the commentary again once the counting is finished)

mind. In his memory. When. Later. John cage talks about the experience in the acme store on the corner in 1935 john cage will think of it. Then john cage takes out his credit card. Then they see him in the street with a vacuum box under his arm. Then after taking the vacuum out of its box john cage's wife will say that he is insanely stupid. That's all. That's all that happened for john cage an astonishing experience in the acme store on the corner. In 1935. Still. A landmark year for john cage. A year rich in experiences. Yet another year without a washing machine.

Minnesota forests *(during this experience john cage or his equivalent will in some way tackle forces undoubtedly invisible but real that govern his personal universe he will have to get a good mic)*

In 1935. After they are completely moved in. The young cage couple decides to have a good time in Minnesota. In 1935. You hear louis armstrong on the american radio. You hear it in Minnesota like anywhere else in the country. You would hear it loudly in mr. and mrs. cage's vehicle if mr. and mrs. cage's vehicle were. In 1935. In Minnesota. Equipped with a radio. The fact remains that john cage is. In 1935. In a car. In Minnesota. The fact remains that he's cruising with mrs. cage by his side. He isn't wearing a seatbelt. Actually in 1935. John cage. Composer. Rarely wears his seatbelt. On the other hand. In 1935. Mrs. cage often drives the car. Great. So it's 1935. So we're with john cage. Sitting in a car next to his wife. He has

(let's say that john cage or his equivalent has a table and that he has small objects of no importance on that table)

opened the passenger-side window. He's opened the window on his side. And in 1935 while john cage. Passenger-side. Breathes in the Minnesota air. Mrs. cage. His wife. Shifts to second gear. Then narrowly avoids a chicken nest in the dirt. Mrs. cage. A superb woman. She pushes her sunglasses back up with her finger. She does this while john cage. Her husband. A superb man as well yes. Actually. Well. Let's say he has something running through his mind. He has a

louis armstrong tune stuck in his head. Maybe he
hears it on the radio. Maybe if he has a car radio
he hears

(over the course of the experience chance john cage or
his equivalent will make the inaudible become audible
through the mic at intervals determined by chance)

it on the radio but I don't know. I don't know if
mr. and mrs. cage's car. In 1935. Is equipped with
a car radio. I don't know either if cars. Even
american ones. In 1935. Are already. Equipped.
With car radios. I don't know. I don't know. Very
well if. It is. Let's say it's likely that. In his car. In
Minnesota. In 1935. John cage. The composer. Is
more likely to have a louis armstrong tune stuck
in his head than playing on the radio. In his car.
While mrs. cage. His wife. Veers slightly to the
right. In the woods. The dense and fresh forest of
Minnesota. And. While she does it. While john
cage has nothing but a louis armstrong tune in
his head. While he thinks nothing at all of this
thing. The hole amassing for some

(he will then delicately brush a feather for example to
make the deafening sound of its different filaments
heard)

time now in his head. Actually. For some time.
In 1935. The composer john cage. Has had a

hole in his head. A black hole that absorbs him. Because the fact is that. In 1935. A black hole is eating away at john cage. It does it without his wife knowing. That's why. That's why. In 1935. Just after his marriage. John cage. The composer. Is frowning. That's why. Actually. Just after their marriage. Mr. and mrs. cage's relationship isn't always sunny. But here. In Minnesota. John cage has a good time. Oh yes. Oh yes. And. While john cage has a good time in the forests. Of Minnesota. In the car. Something unexpected. Another experience. A new experience. Comes over john cage. In a minute it will even force mrs. cage to stop the car. It will even oblige mrs. cage. A

(he will hit a miniscule pebble with a toothpick etc. all kinds of things that john cage or his equivalent will take great care to determine before the experience)

superb woman. Even later. Even much later. To look under the nose of john cage. Her husband. With great care. In fact probably with disgust and care but let's just say with care. Let's just say with care. We won't get into details. We won't get into details. So that. The rest of the way. To Minnesota. She'll worry quietly about john cage. Her husband. So that. At night. On the stopover. At john cage's friend's house. At the house of a

Minnesota friend. She'll have the worst night of her life. I'll have the worst night of my life. She will say. Mrs. cage will say. The wife of john cage. The composer. But later. Much later. In New York City. In a 3rd floor apartment. In front of the photograph where we see john cage. The composer. In Minnesota. At a friend's house. His hand curiously placed on his face. In fact his hand is in the exact place where something. One day.

(of course as in all the john cage experiences john cage may be alone or two or three for example one takes charge of the text the others of the inaudible sounds)

A thing from Minnesota. Entered john cage's car while mrs. was driving. It was in 1935. Says mrs. Mrs. cage. We were in the woods of Minnesota. Yes we were breathing the fresh air of the Minnesota forests. That's what it was. That's exactly what it was. When a thing from Minnesota flew in through john cage's. Wide open. Passenger-side. Window. And hit john cage under his nose. Though. It left no trace on john cage's face. Though. It marked john cage profoundly. It was a black thing. Light. Very hard. She says. Mrs. cage says. Much later. It hit john cage under his nose. Then it must have gone off again. Let's say it went off. There. It went off

again. She says. Mrs. cage says. While offering
chocolate chip

*(while the experience is in process the roles can
naturally be exchanged there is no permanent
position in the john cage experiences)*

cookies from the acme store on the corner. All
the same. When her now old and gnarled fingers
have. Some difficulty. Tearing and unwrapping
the cellophane. She decides to get up and use a
pair of scissors. John cage's. John cage's. From.
Precisely. 1935. When. As a young married
couple. Mr. and mrs. cage visited the acme store
on the corner once. They needed

*(that way the inaudible may take place at the same
time as the text as well as the silences or even
intervene only in the blanks by choice truly by choice)*

a pair of scissors. They needed to cut some
strings. They were setting up in New York City.
They were taking things out of boxes. Like
anyone. Like you and me. Like you and me mr.
and mrs. cage. They'll buy them later. A little after
john cage's black hole. Forgotten for some time.
In New York City. In the apartment. On the 3rd
floor. In an acme box. Still unwrapped. One way
or another it leaves its hiding place. One way or
another it always found its path. Mrs. cage. Says

later. Quite a bit later. Picking the thread back up somewhere. Invisible. Uncuttable. She adds. Uncuttable. She insists. Binding it to john

(the number of inaudible interventions being trusted to fate but not more than 8)

cage. To john cage's mind. To our misfortune. She concludes. Yes to our misfortune. Truly. Truly. Another cookie? Another cookie? No? Really? Really? Goodbye. Goodbye. She says again. Mrs. cage does. Finally cutting the radio. Cutting it short with incisive turns. Fiery. And yet so joyous. Mrs. cage says. Of louis armstrong. The jazzman. The trumpet player. Not her husband. A sick man. Truly.

Mrs. cage's corset *(during this experience john cage or his equivalent will arrange the following or any other similar objects one by one a pair of scissors and something like a packet containing an object carefully wrapped in paper and string)*

Once. In 1935 of course. Of course. John cage goes into his living room. Another time. In 1935. Still. Still. The same day maybe even why not. Let's say. Yes the same day. That simplifies things. That simplifies things. John cage. Still him. Still him. He goes into his living room. Let's say he organizes something. Let's say he organizes the silver. There. That's it. I know john cage well. That's exactly his style. One day. Once. In 1935. In his living room. His new apartment. He organizes. In his new apartment. The silver. So well that. So well that. By chance. By chance. He

(the number of strings surrounding the package is determined by throwing dice it will vary between 6 and 18)

walks in front of the mirror. Dusty. Actually. Actually. In the living room. Yes. It's a new apartment. John cage. And mrs. cage. And mrs cage. Let's not forget mrs cage. They're moving in. It's the first time that john cage. And mrs cage. Move in. It's the first time. Like others. Like others before them. That mr. and mrs. cage have ever lived together. And. While mrs. cage continues doing. The dishes. In the kitchen. In a dish tub. John. Her dearest. Organizes the silver. The knives and the forks already rewashed. Rejuvenated. He goes into the living room and. While nothing would have predicted it. John

cage. In New York City. In the new apartment.
It's definitely 1935. It's not the immediate

(during the entire experience john cage or his
equivalent will interrupt his tale and cut the 6 to 18
strings surrounding the package that will have been
placed on the floor or on the table one by one with the
help of a pair of scissors intended for this effect)

post-war. We're in full economic crisis. A young
couple. The cages. Are moving in. John goes into
the living room and. By chance. By pure
coincidence. He looks at himself in the living
room mirror. Just like that. In passing. And.
While mr. cage. Sizes everything up. Feeling in
great shape today. He's 23 years old. He just got
married. He lives with mrs. cage. A superb and
voluptuous girl. She's 23 years old. She's doing
the dishes in the kitchen in a dish tub. She's doing
the silver. The knives and the forks that john cage.
Her husband. Is organizing in the living room.
Suddenly mr. cage goes blurry in the glass. A
standing mirror in the living room. Huh.

(after removing the strings surrounding the package
john cage or his equivalent will attempt to remove the
wrapping paper from the aforementioned)

Thinks john cage. If things go on like this I'll be
able to take the bus for free. John cage thinks.

John cage actually thinks. The composer. At 23. While. All the same. All the same. His reflection is obviously blurry. He sees himself disappear in the mirror. This is a drama that

(I don't know what object the package will contain)

plays out in the mirror. He will say. Later. In the immediate post-war era. When he recalls this real. Experience one evening. He'll say. Experienced here. In this living room. And once you've disappeared. Once you've gone completely blurry in the mirror. You just have to. Take off your shirt and pants. John cage. Thinks then. At the time. 1935. His shoes socks and underwear. And to make a little organized pile of them in the room and go out into the street. You can take the bus naked without paying. It's possible and simple. Thinks john cage then. At the age of 23. Immersed in his experience. Immersed in his experience. In search. At the time. Actually. Of multiple ways to save money. He will say. Later. Amused.

(it could be that the object contained in the package has an incontestably sexual connotation as the title of the experience seems to indicate though nothing could oblige john cage or his equivalent to opt for this route)

Truly. Truly. Laughing. In the face of. Well. Such stupid. Behavior. He will say. Immediate post-

war. Two knives and three forks. Totally
indifferent. Totally indifferent to. You have to call a
spade a spade. Living drama. In 1935. John cage.
The knives and forks are waiting tranquilly in his
hands to finish the day. Indeed the year. In the
cabinet. A family heirloom. An old-fashioned
wooden thing. They gleam. They smell good and
clean. Marseille soap. Mrs. cage. In 35. But later as
well. All her life in fact. Mrs. cage. A superb woman
at the time. And generous. Loving. Loving. She
uses Marseille soap in flakes for the laundry and the

(but why shouldn't it contain a superb Marseille soap
or any other object symbolizing the domestic order
common from time to time in every household)

dishes. She saves money on the laundry and the
dishes. She's searching. At the time. Like john
cage. For ways to save money. A young
household. So john cage remains immobile for a
short time. So. First of all. John cage thinks.
Naturally. Naturally. He says. He will say. Later.
Immediate post-war. Of the pecuniary.
Advantages. That he could. Maybe. Yes. Draw
from the situation. He says. Before thinking he
should see a doctor. All the same. Before
becoming aware of the drama of the situation.

(in fact the choice of the wrapped object is left up to
john cage or his equivalent)

Well all the same. Before panicking like an idiot. All the same. All the same. So. It's decided. John cage. In 1935. 23 years old. Will go and see a doctor. He thinks. Now he's organizing the silverware. The fine silver. It's from his wife's side. He organizes the knives and the forks in the cabinet. He says nothing to his wife. Mrs. cage. About the experience. Strange all the same. That he's having today. One day. 1935. In the living room. New York City. He says I'm going to take a walk. And he leaves. Leaving his wife. Mrs. cage. A model

(once unwrapped john cage or his equivalent will place the contents of the package in plain sight not hesitating for example to put the wrapping paper and the 6 to 18 strings in his pocket)

wife. Truly. Truly. She makes cakes like nobody else. She's superb and sweet. She wears acme corsets. They fit mrs. cage's upper body perfectly. Truly. Probably. Someone. Someday. Somewhere. Let's say mr. acme. Let's say someday somewhere sometime mr. acme thinks about mrs. cage. Maybe he doesn't know her. There's probably little chance of him knowing her. The fact is though he's thinking about mrs. cage. In fact he's thinking of a woman's upper body. Doesn't matter which. He's thinking of what is. For him. A woman's upper body. He doesn't know it but in doing so he's thinking of mrs. cage. A real woman. A woman. For mr. cage. Like for mr. acme. Ideal. Superb and sweet. There you go. Superb and sweet. All at the same time. A woman that mr. cage. John cage. The celebrated composer of the immediate post-war era. Still little known. In 1935. In the throws of. In 1935. All sorts of experiences. Just like. A black hole in his head. A black hole making him blurry in

(once the unwrapped object is displayed john cage or his equivalent can scratch his nose or light a cigarette or do nothing what's important is that he observes the object with all of the respect and attention required)

the glass. Doesn't want to worry. So much so that. At the time. John cage will say later. I was convinced it was nothing. That nothing was happening. A passing virus. A tenacious microbe picked up from the opposite landing. The neighbors from the opposite landing. A family of 5 children. Something is always running from their noses. Something yellow is always running from their noses. I can't imagine seeing the neighbors' kids from the opposite landing without something yellow running from their noses. Every time I think of the neighbors' kids from the opposite landing. John cage will say. John cage will say later. I remember something yellow running from their noses. That's what it is. That's what it is thinks john cage. In 1935. On the way now. On foot. To the doctor. A guy named williams. A specialist in orthorhinosomething. A good guy. Almost a friend. John cage will say. His dark coat wrapped snugly around him. A scarf around his mouth. Nose to the wind.

A doctor's visit *(during his experience in the waiting room at the doctor's office john cage or his equivalent will sit equipped with a newspaper that he'll wield as he gets closer to the experience itself)*

It's 1935. We're at doctor williams' office. Here we have a cousin of mrs. cage visiting doctor williams. A curly-haired cousin of mrs. cage. A cousin from New York City. At this time in her life. In 1935. She goes to the doctor on average 3 times per week. The good doctor williams. He has an office in john cage's neighborhood. He is also john cage's doctor. When john cage. Decides. One day. To go to the doctor due to. Say. Due to something that isn't right. Let's say a black hole in his head. There. That's it. One day john cage notices that he has a black hole in his head. He

(it would be appropriate in fact to put some sort of choreographed dance or musical theater number at the center where john cage or his equivalent will first be seen wielding the newspaper as it happens the way anyone would by turning the pages you know)

then decides to go to doctor williams' office. First to the waiting room. A small thing about 10 square meters. There are 5 chairs 1 table with magazines and newspapers. There is. John cage will say. John cage will say later. All that's needed for amusing oneself. John cage will say. The composer. A man like you and me. He sits one day in doctor williams' waiting room. He greets mrs. cage's cousin with a kiss on the cheek. Then he sits right next to her in doctor williams' waiting room. While 3 other clients read magazines. They are waiting to go into the doctor's office. The good doctor williams' office. And. While john cage mechanically. Just to have something in his hands. Just to have something in his hands. Takes a. Yes why not. Newspaper. Doctor williams. Well. Enters the waiting room and greets

(then gradually throughout the experience between silences arbitrary or determined by chance john cage or his equivalent will add the noises of heels clacking on the floor to the newspaper rustling)

everyone. And asks whose turn it is. And goes back into the office with the person who said that it's his or her turn. This time it's a little old woman. She has trouble walking. She has a sore on her leg. She came to change the bandage. She came to have her leg bandaged. She came to have her leg-sore disinfected and bandaged. Disinfected and then bandaged by doctor williams. The good doctor. And. Meanwhile. In the waiting room the conversation between john cage and mrs. cage's cousin subsides. Meanwhile. Suddenly john cage plays with the newspaper. Suddenly. Without anyone expecting it. Without anyone expecting it. There is a black hole in john cage's head. He's at it again. He's. Let's say at it again. So that. John cage. Composer. Suddenly. In 1935. With a newspaper

*(in fact john cage or his equivalent could also get up
from the chair and why not do a dance step while
wielding the newspaper)*

in hand. In a New York City doctor's waiting
room. Discovers the musical possibilities. Mind-
blowing to say the least. Of a simple newspaper
thick of course. Thick of course. But. All the
same. Like. Like no other. So that. So that. We
quickly perceive. In the waiting room. That
something. We don't know what. In 1935 we
don't know what. To say the least. Troubles john
cage. Not a piece of news from the newspaper.
Mrs. cage's cousin will say. I know it's strange but
I owe it to myself to tell you. I can't not tell you.
My dear. Mrs. cage's cousin

*(a rhythmic structure mixing papers rustling
newspaper tearing feet clacking bodies moving may
little by little appear to stop to begin again more and
more frenetically)*

will say. To mrs. cage. In person. In person. But
something coming from the newspaper itself as
if. Well. As if. Something from the newspaper
itself. Suddenly. Absorbed john cage. Your
husband. Your husband. All the same. Mrs.
cage's cousin. Will say. Later. To her cousin mrs.
cage. In a cafe on 5th avenue. So. In the waiting
room. Well. There's something like a chill that

circulates between the clients. In fact a black hole. While doctor williams. Well. Calls the next client into his office. A little old man with bushy eyebrows. He suffers from a tumor in his left hip. He limps as he enters doctor williams'. Office. And. Even though the entry of doctor williams could have. At least. Drawn the attention of john cage. The composer. The man literally fascinated. Truly. By. Say. The great musical potential of the newspaper. To the point that. Nothing. Not even the entry of doctor williams into the waiting room. Not even the entry of doctor williams coming. Judiciously. Say judiciously. To break. Say. The atmosphere. The climate in the waiting room. The dirty climate. Established. Unknowingly. Unknowingly I tell you. By john cage in person. The individual suffering. In 1935. From a black hole in his head. To the point that he must

(in fact it would be funny if there were 2 or 3 of john cage or his equivalent so that a game of impressions of looks of relationships could then take place)

go. Without mrs. cage knowing. To doctor williams' office. Inopportunely also the doctor of one of mrs. cage's cousins. A curly-haired blonde. Here on this day for one of her 3 weekly visits at doctor williams' office. Maybe she's secretly in love with doctor williams. I think she's secretly in

love with doctor williams. John cage will say. The
man who. Apparently. Apparently. When he
remains in the waiting room alone with the curly-
haired blonde

*(in the end though it's the job of john cage or his
equivalent to see)*

cousin from New York City. Didn't even notice
doctor williams' arrival or the doctor's departure
accompanied this time by a housewife and her
sniffling and coughing daughter. She's 5 years
old. She's wearing high white stockings. She must
have whooping cough. She doesn't notice mr.
cage. The strange little game of mr. cage. Now
alone in the waiting room. Now alone with me.
The cousin says. Later. To mrs. cage. In front of a
hot chocolate. Somewhere in an upscale 5th
avenue cafe. She calls her cousin just after her
doctor's visit. She calls mr. and mrs. cage's
apartment. It's mrs. cage who answers. She sets
up a meeting with her in the afternoon.
Somewhere on 5th avenue. In an upscale cafe.
She doesn't hesitate to tell mrs. cage how strange
she found the behavior of mr. cage. This morning.
In doctor williams' waiting room. A newspaper
in hand. She says it in front of a hot chocolate.
Served here in big high straight mugs. Served
here with a lot of milky foam. It's mrs. cage and
her cousin's favorite meeting place. Here they

can keep. In 1935. Their hats on their heads. And.
In effect. They do keep them on. So. When doctor
williams leaves the waiting room accompanied
by mrs. cage's cousin. Well. John cage remains
alone in the waiting room.

(yes to each their own according to their knowledge
in fact according to their level of comfort etc. yes
exactly)

Alone continuing this singular and magnificent
truly magnificent experience that. He has been
attempting now. For about an hour. So. John
cage. Exhausted. Literally. Physically. By the
intense concentration that this uh well type of
experience requires. Well. Ends with. Say.
Leaving his black hole. Leaving his black hole.
And. And exiting the room. So that's what was
incubating. John cage says to himself. Once
outside. Once back in the street. It was just that.
Nothing. Truly nothing to worry about. John
cage says to himself. Carrying a magazine with
him. And 2 or 3 newspapers. Impatient to
continue at home. A New York City apartment.
His experiences. It's a good thing he didn't see the
doctor. The good doctor williams. What would
he have said to him. Fortunately he was right not
to worry mrs. cage. Fortunately I was right not to
worry mrs. cage. John cage says to himself again.
Going back home. 3rd floor. At a brisk pace.

THE JOHN CAGE EXPERIENCES

An inappropriate gesture *(in this experience we'll see john cage or his equivalent punctuating the anecdote with simple daily gestures)*

In 1935. In New York City. John cage makes another big decision. He does it in his living room. He does it among his guests. Mostly friends. Some family. Mrs. cage's cousin for example. Yes. The curly-haired blonde. Yes. Mrs. cage's best friend. They get hot chocolate together on 5th avenue sometimes. But right now they're chattering about everything and nothing in the kitchen. In mrs. cage's kitchen. While mr. cage. John. Her husband. The composer. Does the serving in the living room. It's. Yes. Almost time for aperitifs or something. The guests. The friends. The family members. Occupy all of mr. and mrs. cage's available chairs. Savor the petits fours. And no one. In John cage's living room. Could've imagined that. Here. Today. At the hour of

(in fact for this experience it might be particularly suitable for someone to accompany john cage or his equivalent)

aperitifs. And petits fours. And petits fours. In 1935. Right now something essential is taking place for john cage. The composer. In his living room. A man. Already. Loving experimentation. Creation. Invention. In spite of his age. His very young age. 23 at the time. No more. No more. Mrs. cage will say later. Much later. Years later. And. While something essential is taking place in the living room for john cage. For the future of john cage. Mrs. cage's cousin. Mrs. cage's best friend. A first-class chatterbox. Blonde and curly-haired. Is kindly. Peeling. Some potatoes in the kitchen. With mrs. cage. So that. At the beginning of the affair. At the beginning of this unique. And capital. Capital. Experience. Well. Nobody. Whether busy in the kitchen. Whether clinking glasses. And eating. Joyously.

(the person accompanying john cage or his equivalent will have prepared beforehand that's to say before the experience begins built a repertoire of some simple daily gestures)

Joyously in the living room. Notices that. Standing. To the right of merce c. Loyal friend. John cage has a bottle in his hand. And. Let's say. He's taking something like a. Yes. Some kind of. Break. So. All of a sudden. Something. At least. At least. Hits him. Hard. All of a sudden. John cage. All of a sudden. In 1935. Dead plant stock-still in a living room. Truly truly. Realizes that. Well. Today. He didn't do ----,----. While. Everyday. Everyday. Truly. John cage. The composer. Spontaneously. Doesn't stop doing ----,----. Whether in the metro. Or in the acme store. Regardless. Regardless. It just happens all on its own. It just happens all on its own. Truly. Truly.

(as the experience takes place the person accompanying john cage or his equivalent will distill his repertoire as he hears it into moments of silence yes why not)

As a consequence. John cage. The composer. Will. Have to. Within 2 minutes 30 seconds. Isolate himself. Somewhere. Anywhere. I was thinking anywhere. He will say. John cage will say but later. Much later. I was thinking in the bedroom or the bathroom. So much so that. In 2 minutes to 2 minutes and 30 seconds. John cage. In an incomprehensible way. In an incomprehensible way. And. Actually. Rude. Rude. Well. He'll leave. Friends and family. In the living room. High and dry. And leave. Alone. Searching for a. Let's say. Place. Where. He'll be able to discreetly. Yes. Unburden himself. Yes. In any case do ----,----. Without. Anyone. Friend or family. Noticing. Because once john cage begins

(as for john cage or his equivalent when he manages to ----,---- there will be a simple and daily gesture to accomplish such as passing the index finger beneath the nose and why not passing the index finger beneath the nose heck in the background)

----,----. It turns out john cage cannot ----,---- stop himself anymore. So that ----,----. It would be very embarrassing. For john cage. And his wife as well. Mrs. cage. If on a day such as this.

Between the petit fours and. Let's say the cream of asparagus. Let's say the cream of asparagus. Someone. A friend. Merce c for example. Or a cousin from New York City. Blonde. Chatty and curly-haired. Notices that. Well. Definitely. Definitely. Good old john. Good old john is. Well. Definitely. Not firing on all cylinders at this point in time. John cage thinks

(however it's possible the experience be performed solo)

then. So john cage gets a move-on. So he leaves it to merce c to pass the plate of petit fours around. I'm leaving it to you to pass the plate of petits fours around merce. He says. I'm also leaving you the bottle. He says. Already leaving the living room. Already somewhere else in fact. Already somewhere else. At the very least in the bedroom. At best in the bathroom. At best in the bathroom. He thinks going to relieve himself. Yes well there you go. The cousin from New York City will say later. The cousin from New York City will say later to mrs. cage. Her best friend. Her

(it's possible that john cage or his equivalent should pass his index finger beneath his nose alone)

best friend. The cousin from New York City will say quietly later to mrs. cage in the kitchen. We

can't see the future. No one can be sure of
anything. Not john cage. Not you or me. She will
say to her cousin. Mrs. cage. A woman suddenly
intrigued. And frankly panicked. Panicked
frankly. So that. The instant he leaves the living
room and hurries to the bathroom. Well. Frankly.
John cage will not be alone. Someone. A cousin
from New York City. While merce c ensures
perfect service in the living room. Will notice ----
,---- john cage. The moment when ----,----. He
opens the door to the bathroom. So that.

(one can therefore imagine john cage or his
equivalent passing his index finger under his nose in
place of his accompanist's repertoire)

So that. She'll absolutely have to rush into the
kitchen. She'll absolutely have to say everything
to mrs. cage. Her cousin. Julienning vegetables.
Her best friend. A cordon bleu. A cordon bleu
when it comes to the preparation of malt balls. A
woman she's thought however. For awhile. For
awhile. To be badly. Let's say. Married. Badly
married. Let's say badly married. There I said it.
There I said it. I'm sorry. She says. But I had to tell
you. I'm sorry but. There it is. Someone had to
tell you one of these days. Someone had to open
your eyes one of these days. Etc. Etc. She says
again. She says again. While. In the bathroom.
John cage ----,---- realizes he just quietly made a

huge decision in the living room. He ----,---- didn't turn on the lamp. He ----,---- doesn't know of course that. Someone. A cousin. The worst cousin in all of New York City.

(he will announce in advance the instant he manages to ----,---- the repertoire of john cage or his equivalent which could be nothing but very simple clear or at the very least not too ambiguous)

Has ----,----. At the very least. Startled him in ---,----. Let's say. An unfortunate position. An unfortunate position yes. So that. So that. While the friends. And family are. Apart from a certain cousin. Apart from a certain cousin of course. Well. Literally laughing their heads off because of merce c. Merce c's tomfoolery. Serving like a professional. Serving the petit fours and the aperitifs like a professional. The 2 together. All at once if you please. All at once. Wow. While. In the kitchen. A cousin won't stop trashing him to his wife. John cage. In the bathroom. Lamp off. Realizes that. A little while ago. Since the living room. He's decided that. This whole thing that's been bothering him. This whole matter of irrepressible ----,----. In fact this whole thing with the black hole. Because the fact is that he. John cage. In 1935. Has. Like anyone else. A black hole in his

(unless he combines two gestures, one for punctuating the experience one reserved for the points in the speech on the subject of ----,---- it's really the responsibility of john cage or his equivalent to see but for me it's a no-brainer)

head. Well. All that. Well. Makes up. He says. He decides. A part of his deepest self and there is. Therefore. No reason to. Worry. Or. Or. To go see a doctor. For example. To go see a doctor for example because. Suddenly. There is something irrepressible. To do. An inappropriate. For example. Gesture. Or what have you. Or what have you. John cage thinks. Suddenly very calm. Relaxed. And frankly delighted. Yes. Why not. Why not. In 1935. In the bathroom. In his apartment. In New York City. The day of mr. and mrs. cage's housewarming party. It was in june or september. It was in 1935. I don't know anymore. I don't know anymore. Mrs. cage will say later. When she serves another cup of tea. Just before presenting a small platter of malt balls. A small platter of her famous malt balls. John cage's favorite candy. John cage's favorite candy. Wow. Served here in their original recipe. Wow. All the same. All the same. What luxury. What luxury. Truly. Truly.

Three instructions (to be followed to the letter)
(during this experience we will see john cage or his equivalent armed with an erector set old blueprints or an instruction manual to be followed supposedly to the letter)

Once. At the end of his street. In New York City. It's freezing and. John cage. John cage. Yes. That's him the. The composer. Yes. John cage takes stock. We can see him near a truck. We can see him taking stock. To verify the contents of a truck and take stock. While. From his apartment. On the 3rd floor. Mrs. cage. A real spring chicken. Despite the fact that. Well. Actually. Despite the fact that. Actually. Well. She actually has a child. She actually has a child in her arms. She actually had in. 1935. A child. She has her child in her arms. She's watching john cage. Her husband. Take stock. To verify the contents of a truck. Great. So. He walks around a truck 36 times. He has a list and a pencil in his hands. It's a rattletrap with a wooden dumping bed. And. While john cage verifies the contents of his truck. Because that's what item 1 on the list john cage has in his

(first john cage or his equivalent will have taken care to open the box, take out the spanners and the adjustable spanners as well as the blueprints he will have placed them in the right order on the table or on the floor)

hands says to do. Because item 1 on the list says. To verify the contents of the truck. While item 2 says. To give the tires a few good kicks. And he must. First. Go through item 1. Go through item 1 before. Well. Quite naturally. Quite naturally. Moving on to item 2. And. While mr. cage is very busy. Very busy. Mrs. cage. Has gone out into the frost. Onto the balcony. On the 3rd floor. She has her child in her arms. She went out onto the balcony. With the child. Despite the cold. Despite the cold. She says. Later. In her living room. 30 or 40 years later. Or maybe a century. We don't know. We don't know. The fact remains that. In 35. 1935. She's on the balcony and watching john cage

(it doesn't matter if during the experience john cage or his equivalent follows the instructions of the blueprint to the letter actually making the crane or the car or the boat whose blueprint he will seem to be following is not in effect the goal of the experience)

be very busy. And. Suffice it to say. Then. In 35. On the balcony. She doesn't expect. Deep down. Much more from the marriage. That's a fact. That's a fact. She says. Later. Without bitterness. Without bitterness. Truly. Truly. She says. While john cage. Methodical. Methodical. Is on item 2 of his list. She says. So you could say that the old trick. The cousin's old trick. Because. In 1935. In New York City. Well. Mrs. cage has a cousin. Mrs. cage regularly sees a cousin. On 5th avenue. In a cafe. And. While mrs. cage parks. She doesn't know what to do anymore. Actually. At home things are worse than

*(put together some metal pieces any which way with
the help of nuts and bolts basically make something
with these disparate pieces that's it that's what john
cage or his equivalent will get down to working on)*

ever. Actually. Mr. cage is methodical. Actually.
So. So. Mrs. cage parks. So there's still the
cousin's old trick. A baby. She says. Later. 30. 40
years later. Or a century. Or a century. So
nothing is working. There. In 1935. When john
cage walks around a truck taking stock. John
cage doesn't have a second to lose. So john cage
doesn't lose another second. So mrs. cage. Who
doesn't expect anything more all the same. Or.
At the very least. Not much more. Not much
more. Notices. Through her window. On the 3rd
floor. Well. Notices. Well. That her cousin's
trick. That her cousin's old. Worn out. Trick.
Just simply doesn't work. Just simply doesn't
work. She'll say. Later. In her living room. In
New York. New York City. So she can even go
open the french door to the balcony. And wave a
white handkerchief from the balcony and. Well.
Mr. cage. The illustrious john cage. Doesn't even
raise his head. Absorbed entirely in his task.
Entirely

*(in the experience we will then see john cage or his
equivalent make whatever thing following an
instruction manual or assembly plan to the letter)*

absorbed in fulfilling item 2 of a list. He wrote it up with me. Says merce c. Merce c says later. John cage's best friend. John cage's best friend. Possesses. In 35. A truck. He asks. John cage. His best friend. In 35. To load up a truck. To give it a go with him. To give it a go with me. He says. Later. In a 5th avenue. 5th avenue. Cafe. He puts sugar in his coffee with his left hand while stirring a spoon counterclockwise with his right hand. He has large brown spots on his hands. At this time. Much later. 30. Or 40. Or 50 years later. Merce c. John cage. And mrs. cage. And also mrs. cage. Yes. Are quite old. So. In 1935. Merce c is. At the wheel of a

(as in the other john cage experiences this experience will alternate the timing of story action and silence if it is read or acted out solo)

race car. A broken down truck with a wooden dumping bed. Says merce c. Waiting patiently for john cage. Waiting patiently for john. John cage. To arrive at item 3 of his list. To open the passenger-side door and take a seat next to merce c. Merce c says. Laughing. Much later. In a cafe. While his hands. The left and right. Yes. It's curious. Move all by themselves. Without. Merce c. John cage's best friend. Intervening. As if. One day. Merce c will be there. He

(on the other hand in a duo or trio or quartet one can

arrange themselves as they wish provided that there
are pauses in the story)

will die. And as for his hands. They could well.
Continue living. If they wished. If they didn't
want to end. Didn't want to end at the same time
as merce c. How curious. How curious. Yes. And.
While john cage. 1935. Comes to the end of item
2 on his list. He. Merce c. Drums a stupid thing
on the steering wheel. He doesn't notice mrs.
cage anymore than john cage. And junior. Mr.
cage junior. Let's not forget. Let's not forget mr.
cage junior. Also on the balcony. All the same. All
the same. In his mother's arms. He's not waving a
white handkerchief. So he should. In my opinion.
He should. At this time. 1935. Go to sleep. Rest
somewhere between the shoulder and the neck of
his mother. So his father. A good guy. Named
john cage. Gets to item 3 of his list. Opens the
door. Below. In the street. In front of the building.
But on the other side of the road. Of a truck. A
rattletrap with a wooden

(as in the other experiences the duration of story
silence and action can be chosen at random)

dumping bed. It belongs to merce c. We don't
know where he got it. He got it to drive. To get
himself. Merce c says later. Merce c. John cage's
best friend. To. Yes. Ha ha. He goes. Laughing.

California. In the frost. In the frost. Ha ha. He goes. Merce c goes. The clown. The happy man. Of 1935. While mr. cage gets in the passenger-side of the truck. And leaves it to. Merce c. To start the vehicle. To drive the vehicle. A truck with a wooden dumping bed. To California. To Los Angeles. At least. At least. While. John cage. All the same leaves it to.

(a simple pair of dice can do the trick)

Mrs. cage says later. In her living room. Merce c. To take him definitively out of my life. Him. John cage. A tender and charming man. An exemplary father. Mrs. cage says now. An old woman now. In New York City. 3rd floor. However she is still allergic. She says. To truck exhaust for example. For example. Mrs. cage says. When she hears a. Yes. Truck in the street. I turn up the radio a bit. I turn up louis armstrong a bit. Mrs. cage says. Always thinking and thinking of him. John. Her husband. As well as the other. Merce. Missing a gear and almost stalling the motor. Before even the first turn. Before even the first turn. The first turn to the right. Or the left. She doesn't know anymore. I don't know anymore. Mrs. cage says. After 18 minutes. Or 4'33". Of silence. Yes. That's it. She says. That's my whole life. She says. That's my whole life with john. John cage. A nice man. Truly. Truly. She says.

CONTRIBUTORS

Vincent Tholomé is a Belgian writer and performer living in Belgium, eating Belgian food, drinking Belgian drinks, but writing in French and sometimes in English or in Walloon (a local Begian language). As a writer, he has published almost twenty books mixing fiction and poetry. As a performer, he works with musicians and has given readings in many countries (the USA, Canada, Russia, Germany, France, Hungary, Indonesia, Romania, etc.). His latest works are: *Mon voisin Noug* [My Neighbor Noug], his first book for young people, *La mécanique automobile* [The Auto Mechanic] and *Rêves et vies d'Alphonse Brown* [The Dreams and Lives of Alphonse Brown], books co-written with future mechanics, masons, and carpenters. Currently, he is working on *Mon épopée* [My epic] and on a libretto for an opera that will be performed in 2021.

Alex Niemi is a translator and writer. Her poetry and translations from the French, Russian, and Spanish have appeared in *The Offing, Action Yes, Prelude, Asymptote*, and elsewhere. She is also the author of the poetry chapbook *Elephant* (dancing girl press).

ACKNOWLEDGMENTS

Drafts of these translations have appeared in *Action Yes* and *Anomaly*. Thank you to the editors.